D1271262

THE AZTECS

ANITA GANERI

RSVP

RAINTREE
STECK-VAUGHN
P U B L I S H E R S
A Steck-Vaughn Company

Austin, Texas
www.steck-vaughn.com

HISTORY STARTS HERE!
The Aztecs

OTHER TITLES IN THE SERIES
The Ancient Egyptians • The Ancient Greeks
The Ancient Romans

Published by Raintree Steck-Vaughn Publishers,
an imprint of Steck-Vaughn Company

Library of Congress Cataloging-in-Publication Data
Ganeri, Anita.
The Aztecs / Anita Ganeri.
     p.   cm.—(History starts here)
     Includes bibliographical references and index.
     Summary: Describes the history and civilization of the Aztecs,
     covering such aspects as religion, art, culture, medicine, and technology.
     ISBN 0-7398-1352-8 (hard)
     0-7398-2031-1 (soft)
     1. Aztecs—Juvenile literature.
     [1. Aztecs. 2. Indians of Mexico.]
     I. Title. II. Series.
     F1219.73.G35 2000
     972'.018—dc21   99-40914

Printed in Italy. Bound in the United States.
1 2 3 4 5 6 7 8 9 0 04 03 02 01 00

Front cover picture: A scene from a battle between Aztecs and Tlaxcaltecs
Title page picture: An Aztec human sacrifice

Picture acknowledgments:
AKG London Ltd: 9 (Franz Hogenberg), 22 (Erich Lessing), 28; C. M. Dixon: 15; ET Archive: front cover, 1, 8, 13, 17, 20, 21, 23, 25; South American Pictures 5, 7, 12 (all by Tony Morrison); Tony Stone Images: 4 (Robert Frerck); Werner Forman Archive: 11, 14, 18, 19, 24, 26, 27, 29.
Illustrations: Michael Posen
Cover artwork: Kasia Posen

CONTENTS

WHO WERE THE AZTECS?

The Aztecs were a warlike people. They began living in the country we now call Mexico about 800 years ago. At first they wandered from place to place. Later they settled down in one place and built a village. Within 100 years the village had grown into a great city called Tenochtitlán (pronounced "tay-notch-teet-lahn").

Part of Mexico near the modern city of Veracruz. This was one of the many areas ruled by the Aztecs.

The Aztecs invented their own calendar. This stone is a calendar stone. It shows the Aztec sun god in the center. Around him are signs for the days of the week.

The Aztecs were fierce warriors. But they were also skilled in writing, building, arts, and crafts. They used picture writing for keeping records and writing about their religion and history. They built towering temples to worship their gods. Aztec craftworkers made beautiful jewelry and pottery.

THE AZTEC EMPIRE

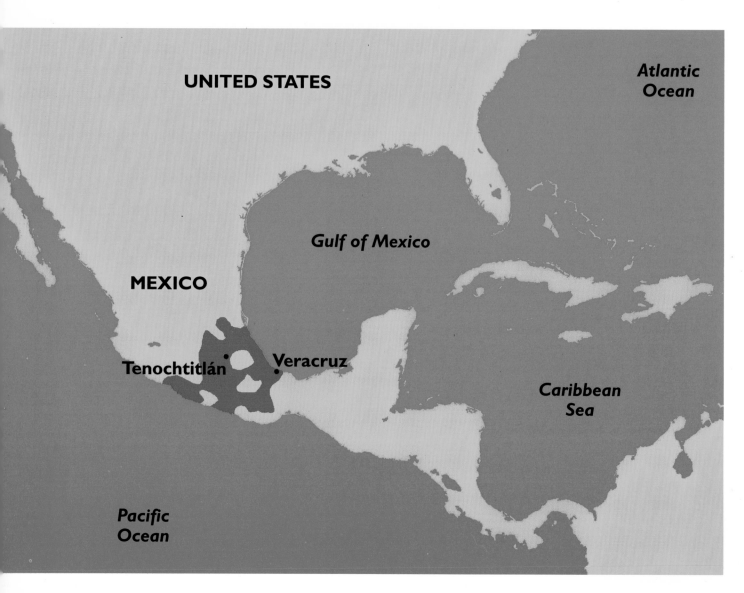

At its greatest size, the Aztec Empire covered all the lands shown shaded in red on the map above.

At the height of its power, the Aztec Empire reached across Mexico. It stretched from the east to west coast. It had hundreds of towns and cities, and more than 5 million people. Tenochtitlán was the largest city in the empire.

Most of the people in the empire were not Aztecs. They belonged to other groups, or tribes, who were conquered by the Aztec army. They had to pay a tribute, or tax, to the Aztec emperor. They did not have money. So they paid with valuable goods, such as gold, precious stones, and exotic feathers. If they could not pay, they were punished.

You can still see the ruins of Tenochtitlán if you visit Mexico City today. The new city was built over the old one. This picture shows part of the Great Temple.

CAPITAL CITY

The capital city of the Aztec Empire was Tenochtitlán. It was built in the middle of a swampy lake called Lake Texcoco. A story tells how the Aztecs built the city. It was at the spot where an eagle was perched on top of a cactus plant. This was the sign that the sun god had told them to look out for.

Tenochtitlán was a busy, bustling city, with about 200,000 people. In the center stood the sacred square with its great temples and grand palaces. Instead of streets, the city had many canals. Most people traveled about in canoes.

This painting shows an eagle perched on top of a cactus. The name Tenochtitlán means "beside cactus rock."

MEXICO.

This picture shows how the city of Tenochtitlán was divided into four quarters. These were called the Place of the Mosquitoes, the Place of the Gods, the Place of Flowers, and the Place of the Herons.

MEXICO, REGIA ET CELEBRIS HISPANIÆ NO: VAE CIVITAS.

Cum Priuilegio.

9

AZTEC SOCIETY

Aztec society was divided into four groups. The nobles helped the emperor rule the empire. They were wealthy and powerful. Most Aztecs were commoners. They lived by farming small plots of land. Serfs worked on land owned by the nobles. The last group was the slaves. They were often prisoners of war.

THE GREAT SPEAKER

The emperor was called the Great Speaker. He was head of the government and army. His deputy was an official called the Snake Woman, even though this was a man. The last Great Speaker was Moctezuma II. He ruled from 1502 to 1520. His name is sometimes written as Montezuma.

On special occasions the emperor was carried through the city on a throne. Ordinary people had to look down as he passed. They were not allowed to look at him.

This beautiful shield belonged to one of the Aztec emperors. It is decorated with brightly colored feathers from tropical birds.

The ruler of the Aztecs was called the emperor. He was the most important Aztec of all. The emperor was treated like a god. Only the nobles and the high priests were allowed to talk to him. He lived in a magnificent palace in the center of Tenochtitlán.

AZTEC HOMES AND FARMS

Aztec farmers grew corn, vegetables, fruit, and flowers on plots of land called *chinampas*. These were like small islands in the lake, built from reeds and branches. They were covered in thick, black mud scooped up from the lake bottom. A strong willow fence kept the mud from being washed away.

Ordinary Aztecs lived in simple mud-brick huts with roofs of thatched straw or reeds. Inside, people sat on the floor on low stools or mats. They slept on mats spread out on the floor. They had very little furniture.

The *chinampas* tended by Aztec farmers looked very much like the ones in the picture above. They were used because there was no farmland in the city.

The most important part of an Aztec home was the hearth. Here the family cooked their food over a fire.

FAMILY LIFE

Pottery bowls like these were used in Aztec houses. They were made and decorated by women.

Family life was very important to the Aztecs. The father was the head of the family. It was his job to work hard to look after his wife and children. His wife looked after the home.

The Aztecs were one of the few ancient peoples to allow both boys and girls to go to school. Boys from poorer families went to a military school to learn how to become soldiers. Some girls from poorer families went to schools where they learned to sing and dance.

Aztec children were carefully brought up. They always had to obey their parents without complaining. Those who did not were cruelly punished. They might be tied up and left outside all night, or pricked with sharp cactus spines!

From the age of 7, many Aztec boys from wealthy families went to school. They studied history and religion. They also learned how to use weapons and fight. Most girls stayed at home. Their mothers taught them how to cook, do housework, and weave clothes and blankets.

Aztec children had toys, just like children today. This child's rattle was made in the shape of a woman holding a child.

AZTEC CLOTHES

Aztecs could tell how important or wealthy people were by looking at their clothes. Ordinary people wore plain clothes made from cactus fibers. Only nobles were allowed to wear clothes of fine cotton and long, flowing cloaks. On their feet rich people wore sandals. Poorer people had no shoes.

Aztec women wore brightly colored shawls and headdresses that they made themselves. Ordinary men wore plain tunics.

Some warriors wore special clothing as a reward for bravery. The best warriors were the Jaguars and Eagles. They dressed in jaguar skins and eagle feathers.

The Aztecs made beautiful jewelry from gold and precious stones. It was very costly, and only wealthy people could afford it. Only the emperor and nobles were allowed to wear feather headdresses or turquoise jewelry. People were punished for wearing clothes belonging to a richer group.

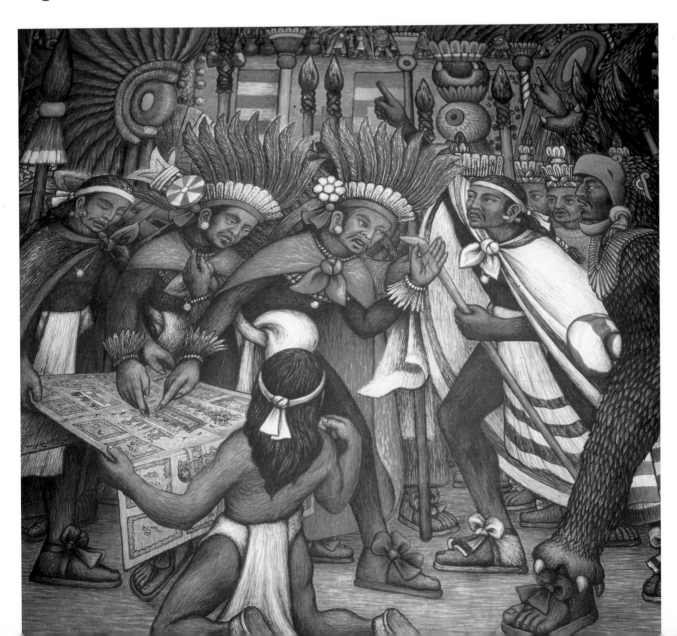

FOOD AND DRINK

The Aztecs' main food was sweet corn. This was ground into flour and used to make round, flat cakes called tortillas. People used these to scoop up other foods or wrapped them around meat or vegetables. The Aztecs liked spicy food, and many dishes were flavored with hot chili peppers.

A local market in Mexico. On sale are tomatoes, spicy chilies, and other vegetables. These would have been seen also in an Aztec market.

Hot chocolate was a favorite drink. It was made from the beans of the cacao tree. They were crushed, boiled with water, and flavored with vanilla or honey. But chocolate was so expensive that only rich people could afford to have it often. Ordinary people mostly drank water or strong cactus beer, called *pulqué*.

This hare-shaped cup was used in a wealthy home for drinking chocolate. The chocolate was drunk through golden straws.

AN AZTEC MEAL

To eat like an Aztec, buy some tortillas from the supermarket. Ask an adult to fry some thin strips of chicken. Wrap some in a tortilla with some spicy beans and chopped tomato. Add a spoonful of guacamole (a paste made from avocados), and eat!

GODS AND TEMPLES

Religion was very important to the Aztecs. They worshiped many gods and goddesses. The main gods were Centeotl, god of corn; Tlaloc, god of rain; Huitzilopochtli, god of war; and Tonatiuh, god of the sun. The Aztecs held special ceremonies to please the gods. They believed that if they didn't, the gods would punish them.

This picture shows a human sacrifice. The priest offers the person's heart and blood to the sun, to keep the sun alive.

The biggest buildings in an Aztec city were the temples built to the gods. A sacred place stood on top of a tall pyramid. Every day, at the Great Temple in Tenochtitlán, people were led up the steps to be killed. The sacrifices were gifts to the sun god. It was thought to be an honor to die in this way.

A mask showing the god Quetzalcoatl. He was the god of learning and the wind.

THE SACRED GAME

Players had to hit the ball through a stone ring like this one. It was placed high on a wall in an awkward position. It wasn't easy to score a goal!

Sports and games were played as part of Aztec sacred ceremonies. The most important was the game of *tlachtli*. It was played on a special stone court near the Great Temple.

Tlachtli was a sport a bit like basketball. Two teams of players tried to hit a rubber ball through a stone ring. But they could not use their hands or feet. They could use only their hips, elbows, and knees.

SACRED GAME

Tlachtli was more than a game. It had a special meaning. The ball court was like the world. And the ball was like the moon and sun. The losing team had to give up all their possessions. Also they risked being sacrificed to the gods.

Another popular Aztec game was called *patolli*. This was a board game a bit like backgammon. Players used dried beans as dice and colored stones as counters. They threw the beans and moved their counters across the board.

Playing *patolli* was a very popular amusement. The board was divided into 52 parts, like the Aztec century.

WAR AND WARRIORS

From an early age, Aztec boys were sent to special schools called *telpochcalli*. There they trained as soldiers and learned how to fight bravely. They learned to handle weapons such as bows and arrows, clubs, and spears. For protection they wore padded armor and carried shields. Then they were ready to go to war.

This painting shows two Aztec war chiefs. The Aztec army was very powerful. It conquered new lands and kept the empire under control.

Every boy dreamed of becoming a great warrior. He was made a full warrior when he had taken three prisoners of war. The best warriors were rewarded with land, special names, and important jobs.

The head of an Eagle warrior, one of the best and bravest Aztec warriors. To become an Eagle, a warrior had to take many prisoners in battle.

TRADE AND MARKETS

Aztec merchants were called *pochteca*. They traveled all over the empire to bring back exotic goods. These included cacao beans, jaguar skins, and feathers from tropical birds. Some merchants also worked as spies for the emperor. They brought information about any signs of trouble in the empire.

The picture below shows Lord Nose, the god of merchants.

The merchants' goods were bought and sold at market. The Aztecs did not pay with money. They paid for goods with other goods. Market officials checked that the merchants charged a fair price.

THE END OF THE EMPIRE

At first the Aztecs welcomed Cortés and treated him like a god. Here they are giving him a necklace as a gift.

In 1521 the Aztec empire was brought to an end by Spanish soldiers. They were led by a man named Hernán Cortés. The Spanish had heard about the Aztecs' gold and wanted to steal it.

Cortés and his men arrived in Mexico in 1519 and marched to Tenochtitlán. They were amazed by the city's beauty. At first, the Aztecs thought they were friends. But Cortés seized the city and took the emperor, Moctezuma II, prisoner. Moctezuma was later killed, and Aztec rule ended.

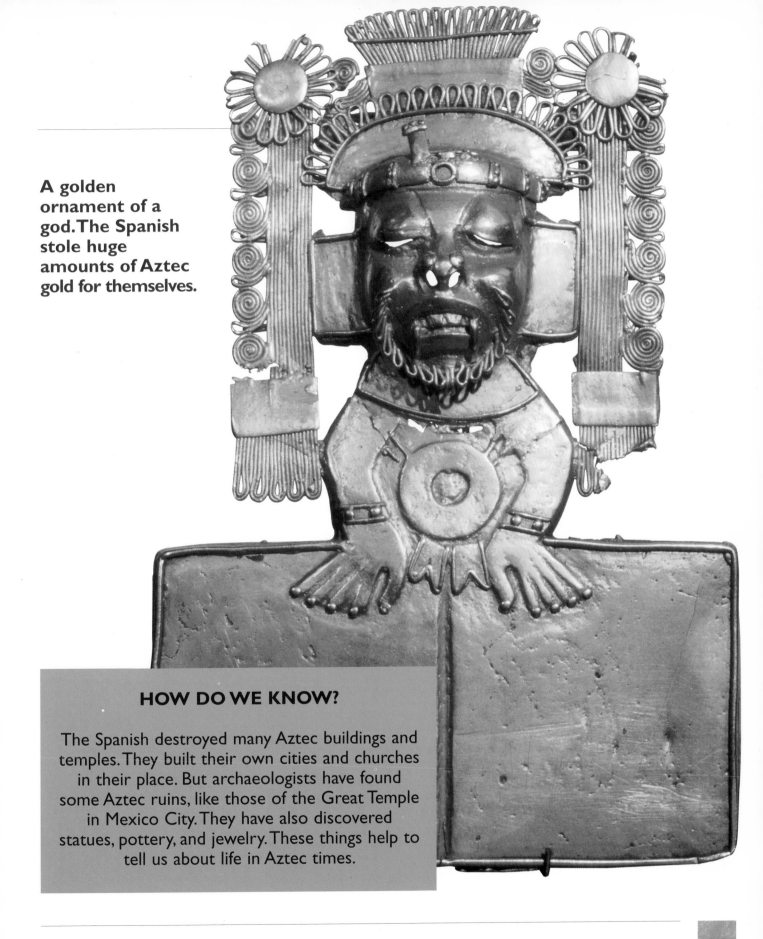

A golden ornament of a god. The Spanish stole huge amounts of Aztec gold for themselves.

HOW DO WE KNOW?

The Spanish destroyed many Aztec buildings and temples. They built their own cities and churches in their place. But archaeologists have found some Aztec ruins, like those of the Great Temple in Mexico City. They have also discovered statues, pottery, and jewelry. These things help to tell us about life in Aztec times.

IMPORTANT DATES

Some dates in this list have the letter *c.* in front of them. This stands for *circa*, which means "about." These dates are guesses, because no one knows what the exact date is.

600 The Aztecs believed that their god Quetzalcoatl died in this year.

c. 1111 The Mexica people leave Aztlán in search of a new home.

c. 1200 The Aztecs settle in the Valley of Mexico after wandering for many years.

1325 The Aztecs build the city of Tenochtitlán in the middle of swampy Lake Texcoco.

1367–1395 Rule of Acamapichtli.

1396–1417 Rule of Huitzilhuitl.

Early 1400s Tenochtitlán has become a powerful city that controls the lands around it.

1417–1426 Rule of Chimalpopoca.

1427–1440 Rule of Itzcoatl.

1440–1469 Rule of Moctezuma I. The Aztecs conquer new lands, and the empire grows in size to become very important.

1460 20,000 people are sacrificed to the gods at a big ceremony.

1469–1481 Rule of Axayacatl.

1470 The Aztecs try to conquer both the Mixtecs and the Zapotecs but fail to do so.

1473 The Aztecs conquer the nearby city of Tlatelolco.

1481–1486 Rule of Tizoc. He built the Great Temple in Tenochtitlán.

1486–1502 Rule of Ahuitzotl.

1500 Tenochtitlán is flooded.

1502–1520 Rule of Moctezuma II. The Aztec empire is at the height of its power. The Aztecs rule more than five million people.

1504 The Spanish leader, Hernán Cortés, leaves Spain on his journey to find gold.

1511 The Spanish arrive in Cuba.

1517 The first Spanish expedition to Mexico takes place.

1519 The Spanish leader, Hernán Cortés, lands on the east coast of Mexico. He marches inland to Tenochtitlán. At first the emperor welcomes him warmly because he thinks he is the god Quetzalcoatl.

1520 Moctezuma II is killed.

1521 The Spanish attack and capture Tenochtitlán. Aztec rule comes to an end between April 28 and August 13.

GLOSSARY

Archaeologists People who study the life of ancient times.

Canal A long stretch of water that boats can travel along.

Ceremony A special act done in a particular way

Chili peppers Small, hot peppers for flavoring food.

Chinampas Mud islands in Lake Texcoco on which farmers grew crops.

Commoners People who do not come from noble families.

Deputy An important official who is second in command to someone.

Empire A group of countries or lands ruled over by an emperor.

Exotic Unusual and precious.

Nobles People who come from powerful families.

Pochteca An Aztec merchant.

Sacred Set apart for or belonging to the gods.

Sacrifice An offering made to the gods.

Serf Slaves who were sold as part of the land that they worked on.

Taxes Money that people pay to their rulers.

Telpochcalli A training school for Aztec warriors.

Temple A building where people worship gods or goddesses.

Tortillas Round cakes made of corn.

Tribute A type of tax paid to the Aztec emperor by the people he had conquered. It was paid in goods, not money.

Turquoise A type of precious blue stone.

FURTHER INFORMATION

BOOKS TO READ

Chapman, Gillian. *The Aztecs* (Crafts from the Past). Portsmouth, NH: Heinemann, 1997.

Dawson, Imogen. *Food and Feasts with the Aztecs* (Food & Feasts.) Parsippany, NJ: Silver Burdett Press, 1995.

Hull, Robert. *The Aztecs* (Ancient World). Austin, TX: Raintree Steck-Vaughn, 1998.

Morgan, Nina. *Technology in the Time of the Aztecs* (Technology in the Time of). Austin, TX: Raintree Steck-Vaughn, 1998.

INDEX